ELIAS' PROVERBS

By

Daniel Molyneux

MORIAH BOOKS

ELIAS' PROVERBS:
By Daniel Molyneux
www.angelofa.com
Copyright © 2015 by Daniel R. Molyneux
All rights reserved.

Moriah Books
PO Box 1094
Casper, WY 82602

Daniel Molyneux is available to speak at your event,
contact him at: drcowboyjoe@outlook.com

The characters and events in this book are fictitious. Any similarity to real persons, living or dead, is coincidental and not intended by the author.

Library of Congress Control Number: 2015900095
ISBN-10: 0692351205
ISBN-13: 978-0692351208

Cover illustration "Jesus Christ" by Ilya Repin
Author photograph © 2013 by Daniel R. Molyneux

First Edition

DEDICATION

To all who pursue wisdom, treasuring it more than silver or gold.

I also dedicate this book to my mother and father.

Other Books by Daniel Molyneux
THE ANGEL OF ANTIOCH

Table of Contents

Introduction

Wisdom has diligently been sought throughout human history. From Confucius' words to the philosophers of Ancient Greece, from Siddhartha's quest for enlightenment to the revelations contained in Hebrew and Christian scriptures, the quest for wisdom has been universal.

One of the magical aspects of wisdom is its inseparable link to poetry, lyric, song, proverb and parable. If all poetry, proverbs and parables were removed from the Bible, the remaining words would be an impoverished shell, largely stripped of their beauty and emotional power.

It is my heartfelt prayer that the poetic proverbs contained in this book will enrich your life in some small way, becoming yet another verse in your own personal spiritual song.

CONCORDIA UNIVERSITY LIBRAR
PORTLAND, OR 97211

Yutan's Greeting

Dear lovers of God who dwell in the Holy City:

Previously I wrote to you about all the things Elias did among us in Syria.

I was the Teacher's companion from his first appearance in the Great House of Prayer until the end of his ministry among us; and now share with you all of Elias' proverbs that I can recall, in the fervent prayer they may aid you in your journey on the Way to Light and Life.

Peace to you,

Your Brother Yutan

Spiritual Proverbs

The Darkness of Evil:

Hades is the home
of all prideful and violent spirits.

Rising from heaps of smoldering trash,
the flames of Sheol
produce heat and smoke,
but no Light or Illumination.

Demons and their minions
willingly dwell in the dark domain,
preferring pride and self-importance
to forgiveness, mercy or love.

Carrying darkness wherever they roam,
consumed by fires of selfishness and hate,
even when sent to the Abode of Light
they remain shrouded in shadowy sorrow,
preferring Hades' fiery torments
to all joys in the House of Songs.

Bearers of Light:

Angels dwell in glimmering Illumination,
carrying Light with them wherever they go.

Bright bliss surrounds the Elysian Host,
no matter where they may roam.

When the Light Bearers are sent
to visit dark dungeons in Gehenna,
glowing Illumination still shines within them,
even while surrounded by Hades' Abyss.

The Lifeless Body:

Life in this world is like
coming upon a beautiful dead body
lying in the middle of a road.

No matter how lovely the appearance,
it remains a lifeless and decaying corpse.

I have seen the pyramids of Egypt,
and the great cities of Mesopotamia.

Next to the Nile, stone tombs stand in the sand,
lifeless testaments to dead bones lying within.

Upon the banks of the Tigris and Euphrates,
mighty empires are remembered
only by demolished and fallen ruins,
giving witness to the fleeting folly
of all human wealth, power and glory.

Remember my sons and daughters,
only your Creator can give eternal glory
that will not rust, decay or disappear.

The Author alone can preserve
your life forevermore.

Only the Source can place you
inside the Eternal Palace
that withstands the sands of time
and shall never fall down.

The World's Feast:

The world is an enjoyable feast in the beginning,
but a painful disappointment at the end.

At the start,
the heart is filled with mirth and joy.

Late in the night,
rich dishes sit heavy in the belly,
wine dizzying the head.

A headache soon follows,
joined by its companions,
suffering and regret.

Learn to abstain
from the world's fleeting pleasures,
or you will never recline
in Elysian rest.

<u>Warning:</u>
The Mighty One says,
"I stand in the midst of the world,
finding many drunk, but few thirsty.

Having hard hearts, dull ears and blind eyes,
they refuse to heed my words of love.

Covered with veils of spiritual poverty,
intoxicated and worthless,
wasting the Wisdom each one was given,
content to be dumb, debauched and desolate,
stumbling in a drunken stupor
all the days of their lives.

Wake up sleeper before it is too late;
awaken from your slothful slumber.

Open your eyes,
receive my love
and be restored to Life."

The Corpse:

Those who see the world as it truly is,
observe a decaying corpse,
unpleasant to behold and rank of smell.

Many foolishly gather round
the world's watering well,
desiring to drink deep of its pleasures.

Too late they discover the well is dry,
holding nothing to quench a dying man's thirst,
devoid of food to feed a starving woman's soul.

The world is unworthy
of the Children of Light.

Soon they will arrive at their Celestial Home,
where a spring-fed fountain flows,
and tress are filled with bounteous fruit.
There they will feast with their Creator,
in everlasting love and peace.

The Flame:

Friends, to be near me
is to be near a flame.

The fire brings light and warmth to you;
but my words blaze and burn
those who revere the dark,
throwing them into a rage.

Soon they will try to put my fire out.

Evil Clerics:

Beware the clerics.

Like dogs, they have jumped into the manger.

Dirty dogs, getting in the way,
sleeping on the hay,
refusing to feed upon Spiritual Food,
neither will they allow others to be fed.

Many clerics stand in front
of the Door to Wisdom,
blocking the Way for those who wish to enter.

They have stolen
the Key of Life and hidden it,
refusing to go in,
while forbidding others to enter as well.

Spring of Life:

The Prophet says,
"Whomever drinks from my mouth
will never be dry again.

I do not quench your thirst;
but it is the Author who refreshes.

Once filled by the Spring of Life,
you must lead others to the River,
that they too may drink
and be renewed."

Finding God:

In the search for their Creator,
when at last the Author is found,
a divine revelation is revealed -
it was the Mighty One who was seeking;
and the Almighty who did the finding.

Human beings do not discover God;
it is the Lord who seeks and saves the lost.

Religious Leaders:

Like a fallen boulder,
blocking the mouth of a stream,
some religious leaders refuse to drink
from streams of Holy Wisdom,
and stop the refreshing waters
from reaching those dry and thirsty below.

Another's Mistakes:

When dealing with another's wrongs,
be gentle and full of love.

The day will soon arrive,
when you too must answer
for all your secret crimes.

When standing before creation's Author,
the judgment pronounced on you
shall be set by the same measuring stick
you used to judge others.

The Blessing of Death:

Death is a curse,
but also a blessing,
limiting the evil
any one woman or man may do.

Judging Others:

Those who heartlessly chain others
to manmade laws and human traditions,
link by link bind themselves
to each harsh judgment they decree.

Rejecting the Creator's Freedom,
not content to live in chains alone,
they imprison untold others,
as many as they can.

Freedom:

The Almighty says,
"I Am the Deliverer,
bringing release to the Children of Liberty.

Even when my Children
are oppressed and in prison,
they remain unencumbered inside,
delivered from Satan's shackles,
unbowed by any tyrant,
free within their own thoughts;
they are unbound
in the Spirit of Light."

Parable of the Rat:

A rat is not made sweet and tasty
by living inside the honey jar.

Nor can an evil person
become sweet and pleasing to the Almighty,
by spending long hours
within the House of Prayer.

False and True Teachers:

Thoroughly dishonest religious charlatans
gather large crowds of adoring disciples.

Using many sweet words,
they tickle the ears of their hearers,
uttering profuse syrupy promises
of great riches from On High.

Beware the popular preachers,
who tell crowds all they wish to hear,
giving deceiving assurances
of manifold gifts, pleasures and joys.

Such preachers know how to enrich themselves,
but remain ignorant of God's Righteous Way.

They are false teachers,
leading their followers astray,
bringing them closer to Hades' Gate,
with each misleading lesson they give.

But true religious teachers
boldly speak lessons
that are hard and difficult to accept,
speaking confounding words
that most quickly reject.

Such bold and obstinate preachers
are priceless prophets beyond compare.

Great wisdom, knowledge and spiritual blessings
come from such preachers as this;
for the Creator's Words are at first displeasing,
when heard by each human ear.

Walls:

Words of Freedom are more powerful
than any fortress or wall,
leaping over the highest rampart,
breaking down the thickest prison door.

With a single syllable
the Lord shatters Satan's shackles,
bringing Liberty to those
held tightly in bondage and chains.

Rulers, Kings and Nations:

Do not trust pious religious words
uttered by kings, tyrants, or
those who wield worldly might.

They worship fame, fortune and power,
but have little interest in Wisdom or Truth.

God belongs to no party or faction,
standing on the side of the oppressed,
bringing deliverance to all people
held in bondage or want.

The Almighty resists hate
and every kind of injustice,
punishing those who work violence
against the helpless or poor,
providing a shield for the powerless
and a refuge for the oppressed.

The Lord is the author of love,
mercy, forgiveness and peace.

Trust in the promises of your Author,
but place no faith in manipulative words
proceeding from the mouths
of worthless politicians.

Leaders and kings cannot atone
for a nation's sin,
or overcome evil's sway.

The unclean and impure cannot do
what the Creator alone can accomplish.

God gives each nation
the kings and leaders it deserves.

If one desires righteous rulers,
one must pursue love,
justice, mercy and right.

If one longs for good leaders,
one must live a righteous life.

If one desires the Lord to bless the nation,
then make it a land deserving God's favor.

If you would change the world,
begin by allowing the Almighty
to change and transform you.

A person's spirit lives on forever;
on the Last Day
all will receive the reward due.

But earthly nations exist
only in this brief present age.

Each land shall be judged and receive
the full penalty for their wrongs,
in this dark age not the next.

Freedom and Bondage:

Slavery is a spirit holding in bondage
the hearts and minds of the oppressed.

But Freedom is a stubborn faith,
refusing to be chained no matter the cost.

Slavery is a darkness
that blinds the downtrodden.

But Freedom is a Light given by the Lord,
illuminating the road to release.

Liberty is birthed
when a people cry out in unison,
pleading to their Creator for relief.

Freedom is achieved
when the people offer up their lives,
a sacrifice on the public square,
preferring death to life spent in chains.

Evil may rule the nation
for a brief hour of the night.

But oppression is overcome,
when the Light of Liberty breaks forth,
illuminating the people's path
that they might clearly see.

When a nation reveres the Truth,
rejecting hateful and deceptive lies,
then evil turns and flees
to search for a more hospitable home.

<u>Truth and Lies:</u>
Children of Light
defeat evil
by speaking the Truth.

But Satan
overcomes the Truth
by spreading half-truths.

Hypocrisy:

Beware of those
whose ideals are no higher
than the works they already do.

Children of Light
are called hypocrites,
because their Laws
are far beyond
what women and men
can completely obey or fulfill.

But amoral people have no hypocrisy,
doing deeds equal to their ideals.

Being lawless,
they perfectly obey their moral principles,
regarding mercy no better than murder.

A Lasting Name:

A palace named in your honor
will soon collapse.

An avenue given your name
will one day be named for another.

Do not desire earthly accolades
soon forgotten and
swiftly to pass away.

Only the One who knit you together
deep within your mother's womb
will long remember your name
and never forget who you are.

The Seasons:

When dark days of winter descend,
the light of spring will soon follow.

In the same way,
when your life turns dark and troubled,
be patient and persevere.

There is a season for all things.

When waves of trouble and adversity
beat heavy upon the breast,
trust diligently in your Author,
the one who can deliver your soul
from every season and storm.

True Religion:

It is better to be a loving
and merciful heathen,
than a heartless religious judge.

When an unloving
and merciless religious person
stands before the Almighty,
the judgment they receive
shall be determined
using the same unloving standard
they used to condemn their neighbor.

Dark Disciples:

Many eagerly kill for their convictions,
but few will die for them.

Those who murder in the name of religion
are the Devil's dark disciples,
earning eternal dwelling places
deep within Hades' shadowy abode.

Holy Sacrifice:

Those who sacrifice their lives
rather than aid evil,
are dearly beloved
and blessed by the Lord.

They shall feast with their Creator,
have fellowship with God,
and live surrounded in Glory
for all time and forevermore.

<u>Winning Friends:</u>

If your cause is worthy and just,
a gentle demeanor and
the strength of your convictions
may convince a foe
to join your noble quest.

Speaking Truth:

When the Truth is spoken
softly with persuasion,
given as a gentle but firm gift,
your opponent may be
led to the Truth,
if they will accept it.

Slavery:

If you are free,
pray fervently for those held in bondage.

One day you may be oppressed.

On that day,
you will covet the prayers
of all the Creator's Children,
even those in distant lands.

Darkness:

Pray for those
suffering oppression,
engulfed in poverty,
and lacking God's Encouragement
to bring them comfort and joy.

Give generous alms
to ease their poverty;
and do all you are able
to fulfill their every need.

Honesty:

Do not tickle the ears of your listeners,
telling them what they want to hear,
plying them with syrupy compliments
of sickening disingenuous sweetness.

When the dishonesty
of your words is discovered,
your name shall not be uttered
without a curse being said
in the very same breath.

Hostility:

A hostile manner
and a loud offensive voice,
will convince many of your foolishness,
embarrassing even your supporters and friends.

Friends:

Treat all people as friends;
but do not be surprised
if they reveal themselves
to be enemies in disguise.

Smiles:

A smile and a laugh
will win many to your side.

A scowl,
with loud, harsh and bitter words
will only attract
fools and scoffers to your cause.

Insulting Words:

Insulting words once uttered
will never be forgotten.

They ring in the ears of your hearers
for countless years.

Creating Enemies:

It may require
one-million words
to make a single friend.

But an enemy can be created
by uttering one harsh word.

Trust:

Do not trust
a religious person
more than others.

Desire and temptation
entice all people;
there are no exceptions.

Bad Company:

Frequent feasting with friends who are
given to earthly passions and pleasures
will consume all your
peace, joy and physical strength.

Eventually their gluttony will devour
all your worldly possessions,
bringing you to utter poverty,
both of body and soul.

Lost Lands:

No nation is more impoverished,
lost, sad and hopeless,
than one repressing
religion, speech, arts,
and the varied expressions
of the human heart.

Revolution:

There are two kinds of revolution:

rebellion against Good,
giving birth to more bondage;

and revolution against evil,
seeking the Freedom
God alone can give.

Controlling Anger:

Measure your words.

Consider them carefully.

Control your anger.

And do not give vent to your irritation.

Hidden within the privacy of your home,
locked within the closet,
there you can rant and rave,
as much as your heart desires.

Spiritual Maturity:

Spiritual maturity is reached
when a man or woman
gives more to others
than they receive.

Sweet Religion:

Many sprinkle
a little religion on their lives
to soothe the soul,
but not enough
to produce spiritual sweetness.

Know Yourself:

If you learn all
the Mysteries of the Cosmos,
but fail to know yourself,
you remain an educated fool.

Knowing the Creator:

If you possess
the wisdom of the world,
but hate creation's Author,
you are the biggest fool of all.

Fools:

Fools are always right,
right in their own eyes,
but in no one else's.

A Blessed Nation:

The Almighty blesses a nation
that helps and saves the oppressed.

Such a land is honored by their Creator,
no matter how many faults and sins
that nation may possess.

Restoration:

Brokenness is the plight
of every human being.

But the Creator restores
even those shattered
into a thousand tiny pieces,
reconstructing what appeared
irreparable and lost.

PART II: Proverbs for Daily Life

Miriam said, "Teacher, you have not instructed us about the challenges each person faces daily. Speak to us about marriage, riches, children, and the many concerns that occupy a person's thoughts each day. How should we live our lives, not only in the House of Prayer, but when at work, in the marketplace, and at home with our families?"

Elias taught:

Proverbs for Wealth and Riches

Misers:

A borrower is bound by
chains of debt to the lender.

But misers are enslaved by
their own selfish greed.

A Bad Job:

Obtaining an undesirable job
is like catching an unwanted fish.

It may not be what you hoped for,
but it will feed your family nonetheless.

Fishing:

Be careful where you spend
your time and efforts in life.

If there are no fish in the pond,
it does not matter
how well you fish.

Small Fish:

Small trout from a creek
are tastier than
large fish from the lake.

Better to enjoy the smaller
and more satisfying pleasures of life,
than to possess great riches and fame.

Desires

When an object entices the eye:

Beware,
its luster will fade
more quickly than the morning mist.

Delay,
wait a day,
and let the passion of the moment pass.

Later,
with a clear head
it may be purchased at a cheaper price.

Worthwhile Risk:

If the goal is noble
and the cause just,
eagerly risk all you possess,
placing your future and fortune
in the Creator's hands.

Pursuing Pleasure:

Risk little for
your own selfish pleasures.

Inconsolable sorrow
comes to those who suffer
great loss in an unworthy cause.

Another's Debts:

Beware my sons and daughters,
guaranteeing a loved one's debt
may accomplish three things:

your money lost,
your credit ruined,
and your relationship destroyed.

Family Loans:

Do not loan money to family or friends.

If their cause is just
and the need valid,
freely give your riches as a gift.

But do not bind loved ones to you
with chains of debt or obligation.

Ill-Gotten Gain:

Do nothing requiring
dishonest deeds
to earn a profit.

Ill-gotten riches
smell of sulfur,
carrying with them
the scent of Hades' smoke.

Risk:

Risk little for personal gain.

Wealth cannot buy happiness.

The rich have no more peace than the poor.

Thankfulness:

Blessed are those
who are satisfied with enough,
giving thanks to God
for all the Almighty has provided.

Material Riches:

If you desire to know
the worth of material wealth:
when the treasures of a lifetime
are auctioned to the highest bidder,
priceless heirlooms sold for pennies,
then you will discover
the foolishness
of spending one's life
accumulating worldly things.

No Regret:

Three things you will not regret:

providing for your family,
giving to the needy,
and living your life for the Lord.

Wasted Life:

If you spend your years
accumulating an ocean of wealth,
your life will end
in a sea of tears.

The dead have no use for money.

Expensive Pleasures:

If you spend great sums
on your own personal pleasures,
the return on your investment
will be never-ending regret.

Lost Years:

If you spend your youth
accumulating worldly riches,
the years lost
cannot be repurchased
at any price.

The Wise:

The poor spend all they possess,
and have nothing to spare.

The rich hoard money,
but spend great sums
upon their personal pleasures.

Rare and wise is the person
who spends cautiously,
saves responsibility,
and give generously.

Wealth:

There is nothing evil in
honestly earning a fortune.

But it is a great sin
to spend all your riches
on selfish personal pleasures.

Financial Peace:

Enjoy the day
without worry for tomorrow.

But save enough,
so that when the hounds of hardship
arrive in the night,
they will not hungrily howl
at your front door.

Pride:

Do not place your trust
in worldly position or wealth.

Earthly power and riches
quickly fade and pass away.

When old and infirm,
few will care what position you held,
the fame you once enjoyed,
or how great your riches had been.

Use fleeting power and possessions
to serve the Lord and to help others.

Then the Almighty will honor you
with everlasting riches
that never pass away.

Sorrow:

If you love riches above all else,
when the money takes flight
and has flown away,
your heart will be broken
and never shall it mend.

True Cost:

An object's price
is obvious to all.

But its long-term cost is a secret
whispered only into the ear of the wise.

Stolen Things:

Stolen goods
are the most costly of all.

The Price of Evil:

Evil deeds
appear free at first,
but exact a high
and eternal cost.

Creditors:

Better to be poor
and not owe a mite,
than to be rich
but indebted to many lenders.

Blessed Labor:

Doing worthwhile work
that benefits others,
is a great honor, gift, and
blessing from Lord.

Tools:

Money and position are only tools.

Like all instruments used by human hands,
they are wielded both for good and ill.

Use your wealth and position
to help your brothers and sisters,
to serve God and to do good.

Then the Almighty shall
shower you with everlasting riches
that will last forever,
never rust or pass away.

Proverbs for Love and Marriage

Sacrifice:

A lover unwilling to sacrifice all
for their beloved
has little love at all.

The Creator sacrifices
all for His beloved Children of Light.

We must do the same,
sacrificing all for one another.

Love:

Infatuation is a feeling many call love,
but it is farther from true love
than Saturn is from the Sun.

Infatuation is selfish and self-centered;
but one who loves truly,
gladly sacrifices all for their beloved.

Faithfulness, commitment and sacrifice
are the heart, soul and spirit of love;
without these three love cannot exist.

True love gives without hesitation,
regardless the cost;
but infatuation takes without ceasing,
consuming all, yet hungering for more.

Feelings come and go, fickle by their very nature;
but love endures forevermore.
Never shall it fade away.

Valuable Women:

My son,
do not reject a woman
because of her outward appearance.

One gentle wife
with a warm smile,
a soft heart,
and a generous spirit,
is worth ten beautiful women,
who harbor ugliness
and selfishness deep within.

Valuable Men:

My daughter,
do not reject a man
for the money he lacks.

A godly, gentle, loving
and honorable husband,
is more valuable
than one-hundred men
with mountains of money,
but spiritually impoverished within.

Well-Dressed Spouses:

My sons and daughters,
do not marry a person
who constantly wears costly clothes
and purchases many expensive jewels.

Your family purse will always be empty,
collecting nothing but dust and lint.

Well-Groomed Mates:

My sons and daughters,
do not marry a person
with carefully coifed and shimmering hair,
meticulous grooming,
flawless complexion,
a fabulous physique,
and perfect face.

They will pay less attention to you
than to their own appearance.

A Sweet Mate:

If you love a person's spirit,
in time you will love
their body as well.

A Worthless Mate:

If you loathe a person's spirit,
in time you will despise
the very sight of them,
no matter how appealing
their outward appearance may seem.

Changing Spouses:

Trying to change your mate,
is like expecting the emperor
to forgive your taxes.

All things are possible,
but it rarely happens.

Good Husbands:

My daughters,
when you find
a hard-working, strong, gentle
and caring man of faith,
you have found a good husband.

Good Wives:

My sons,
when you find
a hard-working, tender, loving
and giving woman of faith,
you have found a good wife.

Lasting Marriage:

If you desire
a happy marriage
that lasts a lifetime,
become your mate's
best friend and confidant,
united together in service to the Lord.

Future Marriage:

The success of your marriage
will depend upon two things:
choosing the right person to marry,
and choosing what kind of spouse
you will become.

Respect:

Never marry a person
you cannot respect.

Once conceived,
disrespect gives birth to
loathing and utter disgust.

Happy Marriage:

My sons and daughters,
the recipe for a life-long marriage
has nine essential ingredients:
unity in faith, absolute trust, complete loyalty,
great flexibility, never-ending forgiveness,
unconditional love, similar sexual appetites,
agreement on finances,
and becoming best friends.

A marriage possessing these nine qualities
is built upon a rock foundation
that shall never fall or be washed away.

Such a marriage will nourish and sustain you,
even in times of trial, tragedy,
and great tribulation.

Dream Mates:

The spouse Providence has chosen for you
shares little in common
with the pleasing specter of your dreams.

Those who resemble your fantasy partner,
may be the Devil's spawn in disguise.

But the one appearing
flawed and undesirable at first,
may be your perfect life-long mate.

Egotist Spouse:

If you marry an egotist,
your marriage will turn and
revolve around your mate.

Eventually,
your spouse will spin, rotate,
and turn away from you.

Entrusting Everything:

Do not marry a spouse
you cannot trust
with your money, life,
and very soul.

What is marriage,
but placing one's faith in another?

It consists of
giving your all,
sacrificing everything and
entrusting your children to someone else.

Immoderate Spouses:

Marry a mate who is
moderate in most things,
but excessive in love,
compassion and mercy.

You will not regret
choosing such a spouse.

Deceiving Spouses:

If you marry a mate
who tells little white lies,
is given to exaggeration
and who cuts corners,
one day you will be
the corner cut and
the one they have deceived.

Making Enemies:

If you marry a mate
who easily and quickly
makes many enemies,
one day you will be
numbered among them
and be cast aside.

Quarrels:

All married couples
argue and quarrel.

But it is how they fight
that matters most.

Unity:

Couples who pray together each day
are rarely separated or divided.

They are joined one to the other,
with God as the glue,
pressed and fastened together
by the Lord's loving arms.

Promises:

Promises to change and reform
are only as reliable as the one
making the pledge.

Like dreams disappearing in the morning light,
a worthless spouse forgets their oaths,
as soon as the words leave their lips.

Criticism:

Criticizing your spouse
is the quickest and surest path
to a bad marriage.

A Critical Mate:

My sons and daughters,
there is no greater curse
than a spouse who
constantly criticizes and
complains about their mate.

Continuous torture in prison
produces less suffering than
spouses such as this.

Historical Arguments:

When arguing with your spouse,
discuss only the item
that began the disagreement.

Do not become historical,
digging up past hurts and wrongs.

This will only harm the present,
hinder the future,
and drown your marriage
in a bottomless sea of strife.

Changing Your Mate:

Do not try to reform your mate.

Strive instead to change yourself.

Once transformed,
you may be amazed
how much your spouse
has already changed.

Loving Mate:

Strife divides,
but love multiplies.

When you become more
loving to your spouse,
you will be surprised
how much your mate's love
has grown for you.

Advice:

My son,
speak often to your wife.

Tell her all your secrets and concerns.

Be quick to hear her
joys and disappointments.

If you listen well,
speaking comforting, supportive,
and gentle words,
your wife will know
she has married the best
husband in all the world.

Creating a Bad Wife:

Beware my son,
if you keep secrets from your wife,
speak little to her and listen poorly,
she may become your biggest critic
and greatest foe.

Loving Spouse:

My son,
speak often to your wife.

Frequently express your love for her.

Kiss her often.

Lovingly hug and touch her
at every opportunity.

In so doing,
you will create a satisfied spouse.

A Priceless Spouse

A wife who frequently expresses
pride in her husband,
is priceless and beyond compare.

For such a woman,
men will gladly walk through
Hades' raging fires,
and face the terrible torments
of dark Sheol.

Devilish Spouse:

Those who raise hand,
against mate, children or parents,
are devils incarnate.

Have nothing to do with one such as this.

Leave them alone,
in the dark dungeon they have made,
constructed using their own two hands.

Proverbs for Sexual Intimacy

God's Body:

There is no place for modesty in marriage.

Be bold and unashamed of your physical body.

The Creator formed it,
deep within your mother's womb,
and knows it's every part.

It is God's will that you share
good pleasure with your mate,
enjoying one another's bodies
completely and to the full.

<u>True Intimacy:</u>

The zenith of true sexual intimacy
is achieved only when two people
give one to the other completely,
physically, spiritually and emotionally,
fastened together with God as the glue,
held together in bonds of love, trust, joy
and everlasting commitment.

A Promiscuous Man:

Beware my sons,
a promiscuous man
plants his seed
in many over-farmed fields.

Each hungry lover devours
another piece of his immortal soul.

As the vacuum grows,
he fills the increasing void
with still more casual partners,
only making the emptiness grow.

In the end,
he is a shell of a man,
having planted both spirit and soul
in the dark and lonely recesses of Sheol.

A Promiscuous Woman:

Beware my daughters,
a promiscuous woman
searches the world for a fantasy
that does not exist,
each passing partner
becoming a bigger disappoint
than the last.

In the end,
her fantasy is replaced
by a hundred frustrated hopes
and a thousand unfulfilled dreams,
as she sits alone in an Abyss of her own making.

Spiritual Intimacy:

Physical intimacy joins both body and soul
in the soothing embrace of love.

To divorce body from the soul,
pleasure from commitment,
is to drive out the spirit,
leaving only a decaying corpse.

Proverbs for Parenting

Parents of Perdition:

Good parents willingly sacrifice
everything they possess
for the benefit of their children,
even their very lives.

But parents of perdition gladly sacrifice
their children on the altar
of their own selfish desires and pleasures.

Parent's Treasure:

A parent's greatest earthly treasure
is their dear children.

Those who trade or sacrifice
the little ones for any worldly thing
will possess regret and sorrow
for all time and forevermore.

Parent's Sin:

A parent's sins
live on as silent specters,
haunting the lives of their offspring
for generations to come.

Spiritual Teachers:

A single seed of religious instruction
planted by mother or father
into the heart of a child,
produces a bigger harvest
than a bag-full of seeds
sown by clerics and priests.

Good Parents:

Good parents
work themselves out of a job,
training their children
to be competent and self-reliant.

Bad parents
create for themselves never-ending careers,
making their children
dependent for the rest of their lives.

Family Foundations:

Building a family
on the four foundations
of faith, hope, love and mercy,
will construct a home
filled to overflowing
with peace, joy and great satisfaction.

Insults:

Never utter hateful words
to your spouse, children or family.

Insults injure more than whips,
leaving wounds that fester,
making permanent scars
that stubbornly refuse to heal.

The Benediction:

My children,
may you continue to walk
along the Path of Peace
all the days of your lives.

May the Lord go with you wherever you roam.

May God's blessing and mercy
be poured out upon your heads.

Be filled with love and compassion;
read the scriptures often;
and pray without ceasing.

Have faith in the Almighty,
your God and Creator;
for the Mighty One
will never leave or forsake you.

PS 3613 .O496 E45 2015
Molyneux, Daniel.
Elias' proverbs

25261294R10072

Made in the USA
San Bernardino, CA
23 October 2015